To Mr.

This book is dedicated to all those who
have helped me write it.

Aspergers is a part of someone's identity, not a disease.

It is something you are born with.
It is not something you can catch, like a cold.

I am an Aspergian

It means that I can do some things really well. I am great with computers and facts. I love science and reading. I know a lot of big words and can play strategy games really well.

It also means there are things that are difficult for me. For example, showing how I really feel. Sometimes, when I am nervous or angry I smile.

Understanding why people say or do the things they do is also hard for me.

Realizing when people are "just joking" is extra difficult for me.

My sense of smell can be sensitive.
Sometimes I feel sick to my stomach
or get a headache when smells are
too strong

Having a strong sense of taste can be rough...

I can always tell when my mother adds
something different to my food!

Sometimes lights are too bright
and I have to squint or wear sunglasses
so I do not get a headache.

Some clothing feels weird to me,
so I will not wear it.

I do not like to be touched by anyone
but my Mom or Dad.

I love to talk about my favorite topics:
math, movies, and music.

I do not always notice
that you are not
listening anymore
or
that you are not
interested.

I am not ignoring you on purpose, it is just part of
who I am.

When I was 3 years old, I was very focused on anything to do with firefighting.
I could talk for hours about the subject.
I owned many books, videos and toys.

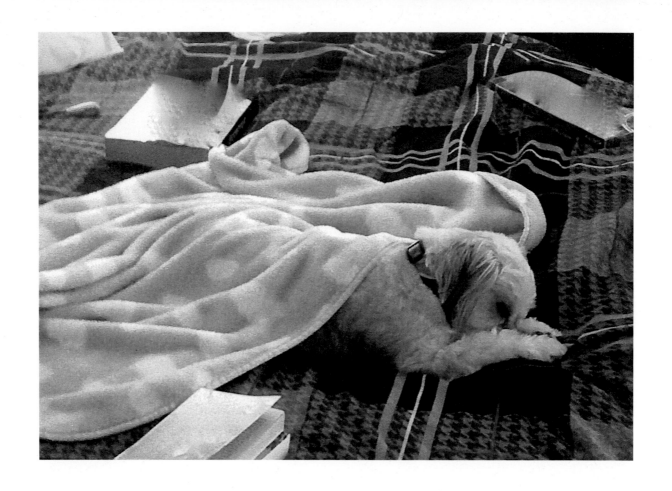

In 3rd grade I talked constantly about animals.
I would sometimes fall asleep at night with books
about animals in my bed.

This is something Aspergians do, we research our
interest and talk about it all the time!

Part of Aspergers is knowing lots of things and using big words. Sometimes I may sound like a "know it all," but I do not mean to.

Another part is that I can sound harsh when I speak. I do not try to sound this way. It just happens and it is part of who I am.

I am very friendly but sometimes I stand to close. I
do not realize I am doing it, so just tell me,
"You are too close."

I have a hard time when people break the rules. I hate breaking the rules even when I am told I can. If I see someone breaking a rule I have to tell a grown up. Most Aspergians struggle with this.

When I find a mistake I just need to point it out. For example if I find a wallet full of money I return it.

Telling the truth is a rule, so it is very hard for me not to follow the rules. Honestly, I am not trying to be difficult.

I often have trouble looking other people in the eyes

Aspergers also means that I take what people say very literally for example:

"Think outside the box."

I can have an odd fashion sense.

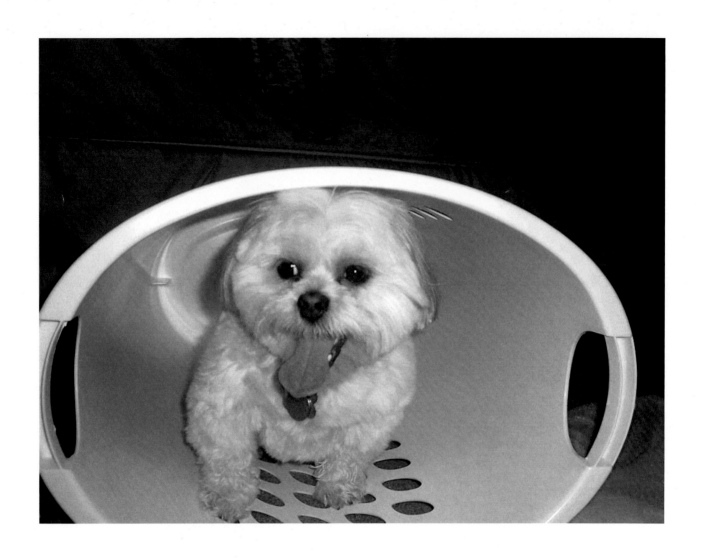

When I get stressed, I often hide in
tight spaces.

I often find empathy overwhelming
and can come across as being too logical. This
is just how my mind works.

Sometimes I hurt someone's feelings
because I do not understand that
what I said is hurtful.

Everyone feels anxiety at sometime in their life.
For Aspergians it can be very intense
and happen a lot.

I feel anxious when there is change in our
schedule, a rule is broken or because I find myself
in a strange place.

When I am anxious...
I get a stomach ache or my head hurts.
Sometimes I pace or rock back and forth,
or I will hide because I feel overwhelmed.

Being an Aspergerian makes me different from other children.

I get teased because I am different.
This makes me sad.

Just because I have struggles, does
not mean that I do not enjoy life.

Each of us is different from one another. That is what makes us special and unique.

I am an Aspergerian, and I Am Not A Freak